WOMAN'S WAY OF THE CROSS

By **Sylvia Hunter**

Cum permissu superiorum

ISBN 0 85231 010 2

Design by Jelly

Printed by Knight & Willson Leeds

Redemptorist
P U B L I C A T I O N S

Alphonsus House Chawton Hampshire GU34 3HQ
Tel: 01420 88222   Fax: 01420 88805
rp@redempt.org   www.redempt.org
A Registered Charity limited by guarantee. Registered in England 3261721

Prayer before the High Altar

Lord, make me an instrument of your peace;
Where there is hatred, let me sow love;
Where there is injury, pardon;
Where there is discord, union;
Where there is doubt, faith;
Where there is despair, hope;
Where there is darkness, light:
Where there is sadness, joy,
For thy mercy and truth's sake:
O Divine Master, grant that I may not so much
seek
To be consoled as to console,
To be understood as to understand,
To be loved as to love,
for
It is in giving that we receive
It is in pardoning that we are pardoned
It is in dying that we are born to eternal life.
(St Francis of Assisi)

Jesus is condemned to death

Lord, by your cross and resurrection
you have set us free.
You are the Saviour of the world.

**Jesus was handed over to Pilate who, because he
did not want to be unpopular, condemned our
innocent Lord to be crucified.**

My dearest Lord,
Never allow me to abandon my
convictions and beliefs
through fear of being unpopular.
Do not let me be prejudiced against anyone
by listening to malicious gossip.
Lord, you know how quick I am to condemn,
how eager I am to please,
even at another's expense.
Forgive me Lord,
and give me the courage
always to do
what I know to be right and just.

Jesus is made to carry his cross

Lord, by your cross and resurrection
you have set us free.
You are the Saviour of the world.

*Jesus began his journey to Calvary with the heavy
cross upon his shoulders, offering to his Father on
our behalf the death he was about to undergo.*

Lord Jesus,
help me to accept willingly
whatever trials and sufferings
I am called upon to bear in my life.
When my troubles seem too much for me,
when my duties to my home and family
seem impossible to cope with,
help me to think of this last
journey of yours.
Show me how to shoulder my burdens,
as you did,
purely and simply for love.
And grant me, Lord, the gift of patience.

Jesus falls for the first time

Lord, by your cross and resurrection
you have set us free.
You are the Saviour of the world.

*Because of his injuries and loss of blood, Jesus was so
weak that his steps began to falter. The soldiers
hurried him along, striking him,
and he fell to the ground.*

O Jesus,
I wonder how heavy
was my share of your burden?
Help me to lighten it a little
by showing how sorry I am for hurting you.
By your own quiet resignation,
teach me not to complain
when things do not go as I want them to.
I am often downcast and low in spirits;
help me to get up and begin again.
Grant me, Lord, the grace of perseverance.

4

Jesus
meets his
blessed mother

Lord, by your cross and resurrection
you have set us free.
You are the Saviour of the world.

*Jesus came face to face with Mary, his mother. There
was no need for words. In this union of love there was
consolation for both of them.*

My dear Jesus,
how familiar you are
with a mother's sorrow.
And how well your Blessed Mother knows
the agony of sharing with a beloved child
the blows and beatings
which the world can bestow.
Help me to experience the assurance
of your love
when I am distracted with worry
for my family.
Have pity on all mothers
in their hours of sorrow and depression.
Teach me, Lord, to show true compassion.

Simon helps Jesus to carry his cross

Lord, by your cross and resurrection
you have set us free.
You are the Saviour of the world.

**The soldiers were afraid that Jesus would not
complete the journey to Calvary without help.
So they forced a passer-by, Simon of Cyrene, to
share the heavy weight of the cross.**

Dearest Lord,
I can understand how Simon felt.
He was ashamed to be seen
helping one whom he thought to be
an outcast and a criminal.
How reluctant the world seems
to help your little ones
who have fallen by the way-side.
I am in the world, Lord.
I need to show
a good example to others
and to support these stout-hearted people
who do help to carry your cross.
Show us all, O Jesus, the real meaning of charity.

Veronica wipes the face of Jesus

Lord, by your cross and resurrection
you have set us free.
You are the Saviour of the world.

As Jesus continued the way of the Cross, the crown of thorns bit deeper into his flesh. Blood, mixed with sweat, poured down his face. A woman named Veronica made her way through the onlookers and wiped his face with a towel, comforting him a little as he struggled on.

My sorrowing Jesus,
what more can I ask of you
than that you renew in me those qualities
so special to a woman:
kindness,
gentleness,
loving care.
Let me help to dry the tears of the world
and have mercy on those
who cause the tears to flow.
Instil into my heart, O Lord, your spirit
of loving kindness.

7

Jesus falls a second time

In spite of the help given to him by Simon and the woman, Veronica, Jesus, overwhelmed with pain, fell a second time.

Lord Jesus,
in order
to save us all
you struggled to your feet
and continued your painful journey.
Give me the strength
to accept my obligations and responsibilities,
especially when they seem too heavy to bear.
And in a world in which so many
are tempted to give up,
have mercy on those who are
close to despair.
Teach me, Lord, to be a source of
strength and consolation
to anyone who seeks my help.

The women of Jerusalem mourn for Jesus

Lord, by your cross and resurrection
you have set us free.
You are the Saviour of the world.

Crowds of people watched the painful progress of Jesus towards Calvary. Many jeered and mocked, but a group of women were moved with pity for him and wept openly.

My dear Jesus,
even in the midst of such terrible suffering
you were able to think of others,
offering words of comfort
to the weeping women.
Yes, Lord, we women need
a consoling word
and a comforting hand sometimes.
Help us to realise how vulnerable we are,
and how dependent on others for strength.
Let me not be ashamed to admit my weakness.
Teach me, Lord, to be meek and humble of heart.

Jesus falls a third time

Lord, by your cross and resurrection
you have set us free.
You are the Saviour of the world.

Now the place of execution was in sight. Exhausted with pain and loss of blood, and jostled along by the soldiers, Jesus again fell to the ground.

Lord,
you were totally innocent
of any crime
and yet you were treated as
a common criminal.
Today it is still the innocent
who suffer most:
victimised because of
their colour,
or their nationality,
or their beliefs.
Help me to remember
that you suffered and died
for all
and that, in your sight,
everyone is of value.
Do not allow me, Lord, to be selective
in my love of others.

Jesus is stripped of his garments

Lord, by your cross and resurrection
you have set us free.
You are the Saviour of the world.

**When he reached the place of execution the soldiers
stripped Jesus of his clothes, exposing his naked
body to the jeering crowd.**

Jesus,
how anxious I am to hide my real self
– even from you.
how reluctant I am
to acknowledge my responsibility
for those sins of which I am most ashamed.
Help me to be confident of your love and forgiveness.
Teach me to have respect for my body
and for the bodies of others,
remembering that we are created in
your image.
And grant me, Lord, the grace to be
yours in mind and heart.

Jesus is nailed to the cross

Lord, by your cross and resurrection
you have set us free.
You are the Saviour of the world.

The hour had come. Jesus was placed on the cross and the soldiers drove the nails through his hands and feet. He hung there in agony, watched by those sad women who loved him so dearly.

My Jesus,
I cannot comprehend
the pain you had to bear:
an agony so great
that it caused you to
cry out in anguish
to your heavenly Father.
And yet, in this your darkest hour,
you gave us all into the care of
your own dear Mother.
Thank you, Lord.
We need her so much.
Show us how to be like her.

Jesus dies on the cross

Lord, by your cross and resurrection
you have set us free.
You are the Saviour of the world.

*After he had suffered for three long hours on the
cross, Jesus gave up his spirit. The task for which he
came on earth was accomplished.*

O Jesus,
let me stand
with your faithful band of followers
and weep.
I am so glad that there were some women
who cared enough to cry for you.
You gave to womanhood a quiet dignity
and a great capacity for love.
Sadly, these gifts have all too often
been thrown back at you.
Show us, Lord,
as you showed Magdalen,
how to love again.
Do not let your death be in vain.

Jesus is taken down from the cross

Lord, by your cross and resurrection
you have set us free.
You are the Saviour of the world.

*When the crowds had dispersed Joseph and Nicodemus
took down the body of Jesus from the cross. Waiting
there was his mother, who took his bruised body into her
arms and clasped it to her breast.*

Mary, my sorrowing Mother,
fold your mantle around all those
who watch,
who wait,
who weep.
We need your gentle hand upon us.
Lord Jesus,
may the women of the world
never betray
the trust placed in them
by their loved ones.
May they be to others
a source of unfailing comfort,
as you are to all who love you.

Jesus is laid in the tomb

Lord, by your cross and resurrection
you have set us free.
You are the Saviour of the world.

The friends of Jesus, having prepared his body for burial, went with his Mother and laid it in the tomb. Then they went sorrowfully away.

Jesus,
you came into the world in poverty;
you left in pain and sorrow.
How badly we have treated you.
But by rising on the third day
you overcame the power of death
and restored life.
help me to realise
that in order to live with you
I must first learn to die with you.
Inspire in me the desire to overcome
every sin and imperfection
which prevents me from loving you completely.
And grant that, united to you,
I may come home at last
to the arms of my loving Father in heaven.

Concluding prayer

Thanks be to thee, my Lord Jesus Christ,
For all the benefits thou has won for me.
For all the pains and insults thou has borne for me.
O most merciful redeemer, friend, and brother,
may I know thee more clearly,
love thee more dearly,
and follow thee more nearly:
day by day.
(St. Richard of Chichester)